Computer Keyboarding II

Word Processing Basic Training Day

for Beginners
and Hunt & Peckers

ISBN-13: 978-1725880931

ISBN-10: 1725880938

Contents

Introduction

Request

One of the first steps in preparing your own word processing reports or documents, on a home or office computer, is learning how to type with all ten of your fingers on a computer keyboard. **A removeable USB drive will be helpful**.

If you are an absolute keyboarding/typing newbie, **first complete** the Amazon book, *Basic Computer Keyboarding/Typing 2 Week Training Boot Camp for Hunt & Peckers and Beginners*.

Mission

Tired of begging and/or paying someone to type your school, work, or hobby report(s)? This basic training camp is for you to type your own group of 3 very basic document reports in Word 2016, the right way--the first time!

Goal

The goal of the word processing basic training day is to help trainees acquire enough word processing knowledge and skill to key, format, and print 3 usable documents.

Objectives

By the end of training day, which can be spread out over several days, completers should be able to use word processing software to prepare 3 basic documents by demonstrating an ability to:

1. Key/type alphabets, symbols, and numbers.
2. Navigate the keyboard with shift for capitals, enter, space, delete, insert.
3. Insert bullets and images.
4. Use the Ribbon to select, bold, highlight, underline, set margins, set spacing. Use ribbon commands to redo, undo, save, save as, print, open, close, cut, paste, copy.

Each report document might take an absolute beginner 1 to 2 hours to complete. Online word processing videos and trainers serve as your online practice lab. Upon completion of the specified 3 usable documents, a printable certificate of completion is available.

Let's Begin.

Training

D
a
y

Part

1

Word Processing Basic Terms

The second step in learning how to use a word processing software program is to understand the terminology that is unique to word processing programs like Microsoft Office Word.

ribbon	commands organized in tabs & menus that help you create a document **Where is the ribbon located?** Open the word processing program. Look to the top of the screen. You are looking at the ribbon when you see words that might include File, Home, Insert, Layout, etc.
spell/ grammar check	a squiggly red line under words that may be misspelled; a squiggly green line under words that may be grammatically incorrect
word processing	document preparation software for putting in information, formatting, editing, posting, and printing
word wrap	text goes to the next line automatically without having to press the enter key

Mission Preparation Practice - Formatting

The **Home tab** on the **Ribbon** is used to format text so that a document will look professional and/or appealing. With Word open, look to the top of the screen on the Ribbon to find the Home tab. Practice by completing each step.

```
Bold, Underline,
    Italics
```

step 1: Practice bolding, underlining and italicizing. With Word open, key your name. Select your name. Go to the Home tab on the Ribbon and click the B. Start keying your name. This will bold everything as it is typed. Be sure to click the B again to stop bolding. The bold, italicize, and underline keys are toggles.

A toggle key turns a command on and turns it off again like a light switch on the wall. To underline, highlight your name by clicking in front of it, then moving the mouse over it. The color will change which is highlighting. Look to the top of the screen. Click or press the I to italicize, and the U to underline. Click again to turn off italicize and underline.

Undo and Redo

step 2: The Undo and Redo buttons are like your best friends when using word processing software. Look towards the top of the screen, and locate the two curved arrows on the Ribbon. These are the Undo and Redo buttons. Click the first curved arrow to undo the BIU features.

Fonts and Colors

step 3: Add Arial, size 16, red color to your name by highlighting your name. Right click the highlighted name. When the dialogue box appears, select Font and the color red from the listed theme colors. Does each letter of your name appear in red?

Margins

step 4: Set a new Wide margin setting of 2 inches on the left and the right. Margins are already preset for Normal margins of 1 inch on the right and left of a screen page. If you need to change margin settings, select the **Layout tab** on the Ribbon. Look to the top of the screen to find the Ribbon with the Home tab on it. Click Layout, Margins, Wide. If you want to specify other margin sizes, not listed, click on the Custom button and key in the margin size numbers that you need.

Mission

Type Your Bulleted List

An example of a bulleted list shows here. Select one of the following and type your own bulleted list.

- the top 3 places where you would like to vacation
- your personal list of 3 favorite spots or athletics
- the top 3 best movies that you really like

To make the bulleted list, select the Home tab and look for the icon with the dot periods and lines. An icon is a picture or symbol. Select the round circle dot list. Begin keying your list. Did a dot/bullet appear? Press enter to make the next bullet dot.

Mission Website Special Training

www.youtube.com   How-To Video Viewing

Conduct a YouTube word processing basics search. Select and watch a video of your choice that will show how to:

- create and save a new Word document
- open an existing Word document

www.gcflearnfree.org/   Hands-on How-To Practice

Get additional help producing your Word report document with these tutorials. When you open the site click on Technology then Word 2016, Word Basics. Select and complete these short tutorials.

- Getting Started with Word
- Saving and Sharing Documents
- Text Basics and Formatting Text

Important: There are different update versions of Word out there like Word 2010, Word 2013, Word 2016. Skills are usually transferable between the different versions. If possible, view presentations that are relevant to the Word version on your device/computer.

> **Check here when Website Special Training Practice is complete _____.**

Treasure Hunt Research

step 1. Open the Internet.

step 2. Look to the top of the screen to find the white **URL box—universal resource locator address box**. If there is any writing in it, press backspace or delete to clear out the letters.

step 3. Go to your state treasury unclaimed property website. For example, key in NC state treasury unclaimed property OR if from NC just follow this link:
 https://www.nctreasurer.com/Claim-Your-Cash/Claim-Your-NC_Cash/Pages/Search.aspx

step 4: Key in the LAST NAME first, press enter or click in the next box. Key in the first name last. Key in the blue search box and enter. Did you find your name? Enter the name(s) of family, too.

Find anything? Any state's unclaimed property website can be searched. Search for unclaimed property in a state where you are relatives now live or may have previously lived.

Mission 2
Type Your Treasure Hunt Report

Type a 3 to 5 sentence, double space report about your treasure hunt research findings. Save and print 1 hard copy. Here is how to do this.

step 1: Take a look at the report examples, page 15.

step 2: With the computer on, open Word by selecting the icon with the white "W" on the blue background.

step 3: When Word opens, look to the top of the screen. Select File, New, Blank Document.

step 4: Center align the title, your name, and the workshop/class. See page 15 examples. To find center alignment, look to the top of the screen. Select the Home Tab on the Ribbon. Look down to the second row, near where the word Paragraph appears. Select the second row of lines for center alignment.

step 5: To boldface, highlight the title and your name.
If highlighted correctly, the words will appear shaded.

Look to the top of the screen, and select the Home Tab, and the B for bold. Does the title and your name appear darker?

step 6: Key 3 or more sentences about your findings.

step 7: To double space the sentences, highlight the sentences. Right click the highlighted sentences. When the box opens, select Paragraph. Change before and after to zero. In the line spacing box, click the scroll symbol and select double.

step 8: Save the report to your own computer. Look to the top of the Word screen. Click the save icon which is the picture of a disk. To save to your USB, look to the top of the Word screen, select the word File, Save As—not Save. Next, select Browse, USB drive. Type a new name for the document like Treasure Report. Now, select the word "Save."

step 9: Print a hard copy. Be sure that the printer is turned on. To print, look to the top of the Word screen. Select File, Print.

Treasure Hunt Results: $1,475.32 Richer Now

by Alan Wiley   Word Processing Essentials 101

It is exciting to know that I am owed a piece of money instead of owing someone else money. The unclaimed funds are from an old house insurance policy. The extra money is going to my fishing trip fund. When I called, I found out that it might take up to 2 months in this state to get the check. I hope the fish are still running good when the check gets here.

Treasure Hunt Results Report

by Peg Tootle   Word Processing Basic Boot Camp

Yelp, I found that my husband's name shows up. I will tell him about this book and the class. My name did not come up. I am going to search for the names of my best friends and next-door neighbors to see what turns up.

Save As and Save

Very, Very Important

Time spent formatting and preparing a document can easily be wasted. That is, unless your word processing software is set to automatically save. But, if there is no automatic save, then you should save a document manually in a timely manner, in a location where you can find it again.

Save As - If you are saving a document for the _first time_, look to the top of the screen on the Ribbon. Select File, Save As and specify where you want to save your document. Save to a removable device like your USB, to the cloud, or another network place.

Save – Click on the disk icon picture to save a document right back again to the same location where you previously saved it in Save As. Be sure to save your document(s) before leaving a work session. It you do not save a document, it is like it was never done. However, if you do not want to use the document again, do not save it. To keep a document, it is a very good idea to click the Save icon disk picture on the Ribbon before, during, and after a document preparation session.

Self-Test

Circle the alphabet that shows the correct response.

1. **Microsoft Office Word is**:
A. a word processing software program
B. a program for spread sheet preparation
C. the most popular hardware program
D. none of the above

2. **To use word processing software**:
A. the Internet must be up and running
B. the printer must be turned on
C. a USB drive has to be available
D. the program has to be on the device

3. **To open a document previously saved in Word, go to**:
A. File, New
B. Home, View
C. File, Open
D. Review, Document

4. **To remove boldface from a word:**
A. Select the word, and press the backspace key.
B. Go to the Home tab, and select delete until the bold disappears.
C. Select the word first, then press the shaded B on the Home tab.
D. none of the above

Part I Mission Complete
Your treasure hunt report goes here.

Let's Continue.

Training

D

a

y

Part

2

More Word Processing Basic Terms

Let's talk about terms that you may encounter as you learn to use word processing commands to add images to a document. Adding just the right image(s) to a document can be like adding twinkling stars to a night time sky or sun rays to a cloudless sky on a beach.

cut	remove selected words, cells, or objects from a document; represented by a scissors icon
copy	the original information or images stays, but a duplicate is made to put elsewhere
paste	add previously cut or copied words, cells, or objects to a document
Home	a tab on the Ribbon to select in order to change or create new document settings like line spacing, font type, or adding bullets, etc.
fonts	various designs, sizes and shapes of alphabets, numbers, and symbols

Mission 2 Website Special Practice

www.youtube.com

View one, short how-to presentation by entering a search for:

- How to save a Word document to a flash drive & open it

- How to cut and paste a picture in Word

www.gcflearnfree.org/

Complete two Working with Objects tutorials and one Collaboration and Review tutorial.

- Pictures and text wrapping
- Formatting pictures
- Checking spelling and grammar

Note: A flash drive is also known as a USB or a thumb drive.

Check here when Part 2 Website Practice is complete _____.

Mission 2 Preparation Practice -   Formatting

Copy, Cut, Paste When an image is cut, the image is removed and the image is no longer where it was--like cutting something away with scissors. When an image is copied, the original image stays where it is, but a replica—a copy of the image is made to be placed in a different document.

Copy and paste the money image of your choice into your treasure hunt report document. This is how to do this.

How to Open Word
step 1: Open Word. To do this select the icon on the start menu with the big "W" or the name Word.

How to Open the Report Saved to Your USB
step 2: Open your treasure hunt report document. To do this, insert your USB drive into a removable drive port on your device/computer. Look to the top of the screen to the Ribbon. Select File, Open. Click on the removable drive location and the name of your treasure hunt report document to open it.

How to Copy and Paste an Image

These are two among many public domain sites with thousands of free photos and clipart images. Select a money art image from one of the sites listed here. The images are usually free for public use.

- http://publicdomainvectors.org/
- https://pixabay.com/

step 3: With the Internet up, use the delete key or backspace key to get rid of any writing that might already be in the URL box. Key in one of the bulleted website addresses above: your choice--public domain website or Pixabay. Press the enter key after accurately typing the web address of your choice.

step 4: When the website opens, find the site's "Search Here" search box, and type the word money in the box. A lot of money images will appear. Which money image do you like best?

step 5: Select the money image of your choice by clicking on it. A hand will appear and a dialogue box. Right click. Select and click Copy image.

step 6: Go to the end of your treasure hunt report. Right click and a dialogue box appears. Click Paste. Click the pasted money picture, and use the star and circles to adjust the placement of the money image so that it looks good in your report. Save the report.

> **Check here when you finish copying and pasting a money picture in your Treasure Hunt report. _____.**

Mission 3
Type A Play Ball 114 Report

Type a 114 words of less true story report about something related to playing ball. The true story can be about any kind of ball—soccer, baseball, basketball football, kick ball, t-ball, or a new kind of team sports ball playing, etc.

Use the insert pictures feature to help illustrate your true play ball story. Cut and paste can also be used to place an image in your report. Here is how to type your report.

How to Type Your Report

step 1: See the two examples on pages 28 and 29.

step 2: Open Word. Set the right and left margins to 1.5 inches. Look to the top of the page on the Ribbon. Select the Layout Tab, Margins, Custom Margins. Scroll to 1.5 or key in 1.5 for both margins. Set line spacing for 1.5 by selecting Paragraph, Line Spacing, and keying or scrolling to 1.5.

step 3: Key and center a title for your story. Press Enter and key and center your name and the workshop name—if any.

step 4: Key your true story. Keep up with the number of words by using the word count feature. The word count feature appears at the bottom of the screen in the newest version of Word. In past versions look to the Ribbon and select the Tools button, Word Count. How is it working out? Are you able to tell your true story with 114 words or less?

Insert Pictures

step 5: Insert a picture that illustrates your story. With the Internet up, key in search words like   baseball clip art images. The examples you select should contain royalty free clip art images like images at Pixabay.

step 6: Select and save the image(s) that best illustrates your story. Click on the image to select it. After selecting, right click and the Save As dialogue box will appear. Name and Save the image(s) to your USB or other findable location.

step 7: With your play ball document open, move the cursor to the place in the document where you want the image to appear. Look to the Ribbon and select Insert, Picture, then the Removeable Drive USB—or what location you saved the image to.

step 8: Select the picture and a 4-prone asterisk star like icon will appear with several white circles or white squares around it. Practice using drag and drop with the asterisk star icon to adjust the image size and position. Make the image larger or smaller by using the sizing handles which are the circles or squares. Resizing and repositioning images takes practice.

step 9: Save your document. Print 1 hard copy.

I Fell In Love With Baseball

by Tim Long
Word Processing Workshop

I fell in love with baseball as a kid, but my father did not want me to play. He wanted me to work on the farm. I had just finished the 8th grade. My best friend asked me to play in the Babe Ruth League that summer. I knew my father would say no, so I asked my mother. She said go ahead and play. We will deal with your Father later.

My coach was my father's boss. He asked my father was I his son. The coach said that I was the best team player. My father started going to the games.

WE WON!

LITTLE LEAGUE BASEBALL WORLD SERIES

by Willie Robinson   Leland Word Processing

Back in 1998, I began to take my great-great grandson to play ball. As his team became older, progressed, and advanced in the sport, we became more and more active. They played all around at all the schools. It was a lot of fun at first, then it began to get very hard to keep up with traveling, but then we got help. As time went on we won the state championship and went on to play in the world series, which was played in Beaufort, SC. We went on to win the **World Series** little league.

Self-Test 2

Correctly specify which statement is true or false by writing the word **True** _or_ **False** by each statement.

_____1. In order to paste, something must first be selected, cut or copied before it can be pasted.

_____2. Save and Save As are the same.

_____3. There are several tabs on the Ribbon to help with writing, editing, and printing a document(s).

_____4. The Insert tab on the Ribbon, will allow you to save a picture to your USB.

Part 2 Mission Complete
Your Play Ball 114 report goes here, or complete the
fractured fairy tale book report to finish.

Mission 3 Alternative
Type A Fairy Tale With A Twist
Just 7 or Less Sentences

What is the best, remarkable remake or twist on a fairy tale that you can write a report on in 7 sentences or less? See the examples on page 32. Here is how to complete your report.

step 1: Online research the topic, top ten fairy tales. Which fairy tale are you going to remake with a twist? Yes, you can create your own new fairy tale.

step 2: Choose a fairy tale to remake or write an interesting new tale. Open Word and type your 7 or less sentences story report.

step 3: Set 1.5 inch left and right margins. Set line spacing for double. Key the title in bold. Add your name and the name of the workshop or class—if any.

step 4: Save and print a hard copy.

The 12 Dancing Princesses

by Isaac Montague McDougal   Technology Intro Class

The Dutch Princess, Juliet Michaela, is a professional ballerina. Juliet danced during grades 1-12, and might dance 12 hours a day if family would allow it. There were 12 princesses' dancing at Juliet's royal wedding to Romeo. This report solves the mystery about dancing princesses' whereabouts and the number 12.

The Beauty & The Beast Candy Bar Wrapper

copyrighted original story by Jaimee Zakia Canty

Check your Beauty & The Beast candy bar wrapper. If your wrapper has a little paper clothes hanger inside, remove it carefully and put the hanger in your clothes closet. Each leap year day for 1 year, open the closet and describe to the hanger 1 high end designer fashion that you want to wear that day. The hanger will instantly make your fashion selection, and it will fit you perfectly.

Part 2 Alternative Mission Complete
Your fractured/twisted fairy tale report goes here.

Notes

_____

_____

_____

_____

_____

_____

_____

_____

_____

_____

_____

Notes

Training

D
a
y

Parts

1 & 2

Complete

Computer Keyboarding II
Word Processing Essentials Completion
http://www.amazon.com/-/e/B01MRY0HZX

This certifies that

_____

has completed

Word Processing
Basic Training Day Documents

Date_____ Location_____

Name _____ Title_____

Signature_____

Meet the Author in One Sentence

Dr. Katie Canty is a visionary professional educator with courses and books inspiring humanity to maximize creativity and/or technology skills at every age.

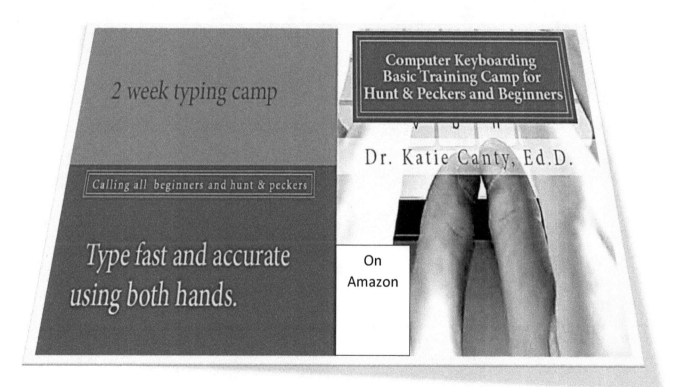